# Unravelling the Essence

# Unravelling the Essence

## Andréa Tynan

authorHOUSE®

*AuthorHouse™*
*1663 Liberty Drive*
*Bloomington, IN 47403*
*www.authorhouse.com*
*Phone: 1-800-839-8640*

*First published by AuthorHouse    07/01/2011*

*ISBN: 978-1-4567-6909-3(sc)*
*ISBN: 978-1-4567-6908-6 (ebk)*

*Library of Congress Control Number: 2011906213*

*Printed in the United States of America*

# Contents

# SEARCH

To find what you are looking for
Reach
To what is attainable
As there are no restrictions
To your options
Only endless possibilities
In need of recognition.
Within the silent words
It has been spoken
To expand the customary
This procedural living process
Secular view shared among mundane.
The remaining cognition
Is left to be discovered
By those who understand what is lacking
Knowing there is beyond
Beneath our glass surface
At an urge to crack through
The essence enduring, awaiting exposure
Omnipresence — the spiritual being.

# FINDING PURPOSE

Patience can express the innocence
Of a soul reaching to be touched —
Wanting to know the truth in a world unknown,
But something consequently real keeps the flow.
Humbleness creates integrity in the less greedy of us all
For what is all will be answered — in time.
Complexity clutters — compounds
What does not need to be left apart?
Not one piece in this pending puzzle;
A dishonest trust keeps the world together
In a continuous motion moving forward
To someday find the hidden most secrets
Proven everyday in the lives
Of us — ordinary people,
But yet, what is the norm —
Me or you?
The beggar living down the street,
Or the riches consumed in material.

Truth—an ongoing search to find
The answers to questions up lining the earth,
But why and what is all beyond
Our life—given to feel
Discover, unravel the essence
Express, and challenge ourselves
Through the journey that leads someday
Tomorrow is another day
Yesterday is already part of history, put together
To explain why we do what we do
And our simple reasoning behind relentless motions,
But if we knew how not to—inherit the given societal wind
We may be able to form each segment into an understanding
Listening to the spirit speaking and explaining
The missing to the innocence overshadowed.

# LOVE IS NOT FEAR

What is love?
Questioning this experience—
Its purity beyond the falsity
Built in the very word
Expressed by those who try to claim to love
As love should be,
But the language and motions of this action
External to the actual emotion
Bear claims of false pretence
Untrue to those who understand
That love is not violent or jealous ruptures
Do not wait to find the true meaning of the feeling, love.

# STRONG COURAGE, GROW STRONGER

Little girl
Why does she sit there — still
Her hair straying long in frayed knots
Eyes puffy and swollen
Blue and black.
Little girl
Why does she sit there — still
Her undeveloped hands known too far into this world
Her body limb to fall
Bony, breast less
Little girl
Is there a woman forming inside of you?
How will you figure into this world?
The project concept — I wonder
As she watches — as I stare
Back into her eyes
Little girl
Why do you sit there and smile?

# LIFELONG

My acceptance of you
Was far away
With distorted thoughts
Leaving me alone
Through your understanding.
Your desperation
To find a simple recognition
Has just brought on
A loss of feeling between both.
The spring to a new season
Has seemed to let your fear down
And lost cries let go.
I believe your apprehension
Has brought itself into extinction
And you felt the need
To silently admit, you were wrong.

# WHICH WAY

Turning point again
Left or right?
Because the guidance has not been directed,
Or simply not heard.
Lost—in a path of vicarious lesions
Which step is the correct move ahead,
Or is one necessarily right?
In comparison to another—trust in transformation
Because the wave is winding, turning again
Impeding on—and I cannot keep up.

# THE KEY IS LOCKED

Where do I belong?
In this disarray
Lost in the translation
Of your words unspoken
And your actions felt to predict
The creation of our attraction.
A rarity bond building on forbidden love
Wanting to be set free
Like birds expressing spring serenity
As you are to me
And those eyes that strike like crystals
Matching the shinning of the sun
You are to me, and if only
I can be this close please
Not drift further away as seasons change
Just keep me warm like this summer, and pause my time
In these unforgettable moments made memories.

# MENDED

Too often we have found ourselves
Holding our lives with he or she
Only to fill an empty void
That another he or she has pierced
The wounded heart.
As the pattern is played pretend for the purpose
Occupying the mind, patch the heart
If the void is no longer
The imaginary potentially to become a reality.

# FIND YOURSELF

Was once told
Before you even attempt
To find someone else
Know yourself
Reveal what is inside
Be your own best friend
Before you can fill that role
To someone else
Identify the identity
Beyond the scratched surface
Ask yourself the question
Who am I?

# HER MISUNDERSTANDING

Satin sheets covered upon her body
The morning she watched him try
Filling the empty cup
Counting paper that will lead
To a place she had not wanted to know.
Feathered pillows ruffled
And pleasantly kept her comfort
The morning his ciggie kept the fixation
Of his earnings — what he felt
Was the meaning.
And she was not thankful
For these many blankets
Illusioned to keep her safe,
Although created the warmth that held her against him.
In response to observing
She emptied the change she had inside
And it meant so much — worth so much more
Than these satin sheets and empty cup filled
Could ever amount to.

# ALTRUISTIC DISCOVERY

Meander to the way the world walks
Until the connotation can be brought about.
A discovery of one's self—
Simple in comparison to the entire.
The understanding of eternity—
A resolution to the soulful disposition
A credence that few contend to conform with
The formality that should already be.
Why wait until the end to reach the beginning
When this journey has already begun?
The human mind perceived linear,
Why have we discarded the dimensions?
A fraction, a portion is not the whole
But an element of our totality
So many seem to miss.

Why care for yourself
If you cannot care for others?
A drive to self destruction
The course of individuals colliding.
An equal basis
Is not half humanity
Stricken with starvation
Social determinants restricting survival.
An ingrained universal conviction to formulate
All footprints to function accordingly
Has continued to be accepted,
A new notion in need to be distinguished
Before the global race
Extinguished.

# IN LOVE FALLING OUT

Why did the tide flow in?
As the rocky waves lingered,
Slowly through the stepping stones on shore
Grasping on hard, never to let go.
Why did the tide flow in?
When it did not know its way, and floated
Lost in the shallowness of understanding
Found only deep within the wading pools,
When the tide flew in
And the waves still lingered.

# BAD REWIND

Subconsciously
The pictures set in mind
In a dark resting period
Hours before dawn
It began.
A flood of emotion: fear
Over powered mind, body in trickery
Feeling as though it was real —
It was then, but not now.
Reminded in terrors that taunt
In the night, sneaking in a trying sleep —
Overthrown by panic,
Captions running fast as frighten thoughts push through
Trying to escape from past moments —
Now memories as nightmares,
Unlike the actual actions
That once struck so strong —
Hours before dawn
Routinely as it began.

# THE BUILDER

To design his forth coming
He structures the tangible
As the work thrives him to go on.
Succeed amongst simplicity
The wood made to lumber
His creation — other's foundation.
Within the home survival prepared
Shared on this timber table
Giving thanks to our nation's nature
The essence — created formation
Deliver in appreciation.

# CREATED RIVALRY

I am a piece
You attempt to move
In your game called life.
I will fight to be the knight
Yet the strategic pawns
You set against me
Off set a ratio
As a challenge to identify
Realities of masked bodies.
The tricks, the gimmicks
I do not play back
Work is not a game
In any case
You already lost.

# EMBRACE

Let me tell you
Whisper the pureness
Of a truth so real
What became, and is
I always dreamed to be.
Let me get lost
In your eyes so deep
In a journey so far
So close together
I can feel it.
Let me show you
Take my hand, feel
My heart—the continual pounding
The extra beat
Close as two, we became one.
Let me express to you
This notion—I've been hanging onto a verge of purity
Where I am falling more and more
In love, and there is not anything else
It is you—has completed me.

# AS THE STORY IS TOLD

Lightening struck you
Exactly on the wedding ring
That marked a delay in your future—
Ever the thought that the entire
Marriage of false promises
Was a small step in the broad journey
So your life
Did not have to end early?

# ARE YOU THE ONE?

Your eyes tell stories of possibilities
Reaching out to be found.
Am I meant to discover
Disentangle what is inside—a providence to be revealed?
Is now the time to look into the eyes
Of my one half—missing?
Correct in judgement or a dealing of deception,
Questions will not exist
When the answers remain
Understanding that my destiny
Must not be—your own.

# BELIEVING

Bodies of the norm as creatures we roam
Unreceptive to the pathway
Instead monotonous movements
Daily patterns to calculate an entire life capsule.
Global race divided
In countless divisions, one difference
Those who believe differently
The meaning of what is.
Fortune, fame
Materialism, money
Power
Publicity, popularity
Love competing lust
Ruling religions, rather
Belief in a higher being
Reaching the awaiting eternity
Found meaning.

# ACCEPTANCE

Can I please?
Exist in your world — I now know
My presence does not belong
In this fiction you know,
In what you understand
The barriers to be, and to me
Only endless possibilities.
Can I cross the boundary?
Break the constraint
Create an acknowledgement
For the undisclosed,
Or will you keep that change —
Chance confined?
Conform to restrictions and accept the unacceptance
I cannot continue to comply to the restraints that apply
Abiding to against what is true
What is real, what could be forever?

# IN YOUR SHOES

If I stepped
Into your shoes
Maybe then—
Only then
Could I understand
Why
You do what you do
And appreciate it
Just the same.

# NO NEED TO CONINCIDE

Consider the prism — the dimensions of our survival
The average conceptualizing in three,
Although the common eye cannot detect the truth
This does not eliminate reality.
What many pose in a naive state
Is a false belief in a concrete form.
The human race
Surviving off the feed of each other
North drenched in riches — a material masquerade
South left to suffer and fend in fertile death — division created
Should not have existed
Yet global plagues pushed power —
Instead demand passion for positive policy
Teach the truth
In what you are taught.

# GRASP ON

You stole my heart
That I never considered giving away
Hanging on so tight
To let you not
Know who really is behind the
Face you called beautiful
That I never knew.
And there was that moment
Where it could have been prevented
But I lost the strength
To clutch against a fear
For the desire of your love
To know what it truly means
And what that could reveal.

# INNOCENT

A child cries out
Among all bearings, and the little
One shakes when no one responds.
Hiding
Is the best friend
Well known to the world
When all else is at loss
Crying
The tears through a soul
That can never breathe
Smothers down all
Recognition
Found through fear
Of an unspoken truth
A young child marks innocence
As grown the spoken now heard.

# WITHIN CREATION

Each embodiment holds all accessible knowledge
Inner desires that need to be explored
Truthful thoughts waiting to be outspoken
Expandable actions to alleviate the unjust.
One has the power to make the decision
Find answers defining the missing
Piece in forming utopia, you and I — together
As a nation it should be built
On minimum for the sake of global survival.
Possible premise of the problem — each one of us
Swarmed — engulfed within the box
Not ever considering beyond the usual
File to follow one as one
A difference possible with instinct to change
Knowing that there are no limits
And what is set
Is own self restriction
Reverse with conviction.

# ELECTRICITY

He held me ever so close
As I drew near to the sweetness of his embrace
Listening to the silent words played
Through from his spirit to my soul
Mate, I have found you
Whispering the gentles through
My body as single moments
Paused to feel the urge
To know you more
As every part
Made a whole
Inside my fragile self
And then our lips softly closed in
On each other's felt emotion
Into an intimate world of passion
Defining forever yearning devotion.

# FAITH

Her soul is like a broken wing
They struggle and those seek to make her believe
The vengeance pushed upon
A woman so ultimately small
To the force of aggression
Brought on by deception.
All swallow around the softness of her being
And she cannot be let free
Rashness bites hard on to
The convexity — brought life.
Faithful prayer —
Grace gives freedom
The refinement — light a soul
And soar above those who sneak
With effort for her to accept
A continual adverse line of attack.
Trust in the essence — the wings peace together
The missing steps of a human footprint
Trust in the inner voice, hold hope
Rescued to the other side.

# CONQUER THE QUEST

The hours that made days
What did the years leave behind?
For too many — chances not taken
Feelings sadly dismissed, the guilt that left residue
On hearts done wrong
Now wanting to correct broken promises
Continuous possibilities as unused potential
Rewind to opportunities discarded.
A life time now at the brink of termination
Sudden awareness, the essence to be revealed
In the final moments ever so clear
Do not wait until the end to find the beginning
Believe and conquer, discover beyond creation
Do not miss on what should not be forgotten.

# FIRST TIME

When I felt the softness of your lips
I melted warm. It was not right
For me to love those lips so much
And I could not help myself
To kiss them just once more.
Pause to find that second breath
The first you took away —
Affirm my assumptions
Or at least for this very moment
Let me believe what I feel is what you want.

# RIBBON ROAD

Music fills the empty space
Drives on with the wind in her face
Sudden stop
The man on her right shouts out
Green — go
She speeds — passing images
Like a flip book movie
Deja vu scenes call out in a voice
Once easily recognised — affliction fills
The young in minded
Stop the past
This is now present — future
The wind in her face
Calms, music fills the empty space.

# TEMPTATION

What other option existed
If I did not have the choice
But to say goodbye to the pure beauty
Struck inside, shining outside your presence.
How could I go without?
The drink of life — as water to the body
You are to my spirit.
This desire has become a recognised need
For what I know is real,
Capsizing on my thoughts to turn away
On what is right — circumstantially determined wrong.

*Andréa Tynan*

# ONE BY ONE

Life is a mystery
Of unexplained occurrences
That haunt our lives
Unhappiness, grief
Death that does not do us part
Forever is not always.

# PERMISSIBLE

If I knew real love
I would say it was inside you
Just waiting to get out—be set free
As it awaits so do I
Will you allow a future unknown—
Can it be known?
Home
Where your heart has found
Its bearings
Not glued on the globe.
I understand they do not approve
I am aware of your words
But your eyes distinctly say otherwise.

# DARING FOR THE DIFFERENCE

It is your right to question
To defy logic
A scientific knowledge
Assumed as the truth.
Those who inquire find answers
To the underlying reality
Revealed to those who search
In the path of purity.
What will hold up human frailty
Is not the science labelled solid
Rather the faith one discovers
In a struggling maze
Labelled life.

Brought to us, a jigsaw
Some the puzzle—missing pieces,
Others having everything
Not giving anything
And painfully realizing they have nothing.
A tunnel scoped to those who reach
Beyond the apparent
Make a glimpse at touching
What is real?
Until appreciating what is real
Is unable to be touched.

# WHEN EVERYTHING IS STILL

Sometimes I miss
Him when everything is quiet
A distant emptiness
Holding nothing beside me
As I sleep his body once held me
Safe, structured in a routine of familiarity
But what I knew is gone
I had to say goodbye
Decipher between habit
And what is love.

# TRUTH LET OUT

To be fearless yet scared?
Silencing the question, when God spoke: be brave.
Listening to these words, realizing — unable to live a lie
And expect to tell the truth.
Prior — successful in stating
A supporting idea of splendid-false patterns
Continuously slurred off as vocal repetition
Now forbidden — fatal memories exposed
Truth found — and to be recorded as sound
Acknowledged as a fallacy.

# FEAR DOES NOT BELONG

Afraid
To love you
To hurt
The heart
Damaged.
Scared
To trust
The words
You pull
And push
My way.
Fear
Is holding back
Eliminating a possible love
Yet wishing and wanting so bad
And knowing that it
Can never be.

# GO WITH THE FLOW

When it is the only thing you know
Trace your steps into a cathedral
Let it know you.
Teach to humble yourself
When you are selfish
Plead by your mercy
When your self has left you defeated.
Let the sightless guide you
A golden path to selflessness.
Follow your footsteps
Until they leave a mark
Carry those who are unable to do so.

# THE AFTERMATH

Sitting still together
Waiting to hear the voice
Once known so well
Listening to the silence
And feeling your thoughts,
But where were you
When I called out your name
And you could not call back but holler out loud
The anger that stays inside
Keeping you alive.
But I am not that guy
I promise.
Please never promise
Aware of what cannot be kept.

# SHE IS LOST

And I found her
In some guy's car. But
This isn't a guy you would
Picture her with
He's wearing pyjama pants
A t-shirt that seems known to well
A drained face and worn eyes — shaggy hair
Long pony tail
He seems harmless
What could he want? Her
Body- unaware
She should not be there.

# PAUSE TIME

Light spirited, no stress existing
In this world where we know it all too well
A feeling of euphoria, not known before.
To capture a sensation as everlasting
An overall peace of comfort to share — to be in love
To feel what was once the unknown
And hung as a desperation plea
No words were needed to express
A desire for something more
Solitude struck severely
And silence is not heard.
An authentic man
Holding happiness in his hand
Created fascination to discovery
Capture these minutes
May be all that is given
Cherish this moment, magnetize in momentum.

# DISCOVERY

Realizing where you went wrong
Frontier
The day the battle began
Search
A maze through the mind
Questions
Potentially to answer the truth
Proclaim
A triumph of a lighted chest
Discovery
Knowing you did everything right.

# TELLING A LYE

It is beyond the eyes that the truth is told
An unconscious willingness to show through
In mini crystal balls — a backward reality
Presented as a true account
At the end — the bitter end, the salt tasted
And any recount retold correctly.
Honesty as it burns
Stings through open wounds
Nestled in the cracks of aging bones
Punctures to the heart
The crystals tainted steel
The sparkle stained.

# THE ARRIVAL

Adventure the undone

For the essence will come

This time is change, and day is loosing

Against the dark of night of what is above or below

Scared nature held in between the ways

Good, evil, a new age is approaching

Pacing to the ending

A silent movement is slowly drawing in

As a clear not seen ghost of day

Searching to recognize its catch or prey

Act is to be

The way of the not to see

Do not follow in command

A question of none

The mother earth spiralling winding down

With no choice but to crash

The storms of night brewing

A global race in destruction

Watch as we wait—the arrival the end.

*Andréa Tynan*

# TWO LIVES

We stopped at the sight
Of the rounded red traffic light
The next lane car — an older lady
Slapped across her face in her hands
Tears melting down rouge cheeks
Her spouse — or so it seemed he was
Eyes fixed on the red, hands clutched on the wheel
Green we started off —
Left behind — now witnesses of a caption
A chapter in the story, a paragraph in the page
One line in the life of the unnamed.

# MIRROR IMAGE

Gaze with persistence through the mirror
An image I believe is me
Staring back looking through the eyes
That hide the inside
Self behind an outside solid shell, could it be?
Questioning notions of past judgment
Wishing for answers, debating if there is
Simpler resolutions, than I had come to acknowledge
Did the solid shell shatter?
I see a different person in the mirror
Then I feel inside, of whom could it be?
Me, it is who I see.

# LOVE

Is the only fixation of a resemblance
As something whole in this world
Through an unexplained journey
That leads nowhere to some
To somewhere so much greater to others.
Where would life take us is we have not loved
The innocence of another presence
If you have never been loved by the loving
Or in love — would be going through an exploration of life missing
A part of another and having a part of yourself
Absent from the rest of your being
A reality behind the word that is too often misplaced.

# WHO ARE YOU?

Cannot find answers to the questions that drift
Into your mind concerning
And wondering as to what you are thinking
Empathise with you, appears you are hiding your life
Not wanting anyone to know
What happened to you?
That crumbled your soul from the inside out
Hard to hide and illustrate on the surface
A smile smeared sham, a fear
For no one will accept you into society
Even though they have, but not the real you.

# DO NOT DENIE

May love be stronger?
Than a present fear or the denial that
Separates the two.
What is wrong — trying to love with apprehension
Hesitation against the truth
For love is pure — bona fide
Honest, perfect, love is complete;
Therefore the remaining question —
What is the root of this tree?
Too afraid to be planted.

# RESCUED

She who became possessed
Latching on hard
To which she will never have.
He eliminated the sorcerer
The builder to rebuild
From ground surface with no ceiling.
Little she grew quick into the world
Of known which should have been unknown,
Now the little she needed him
In a glimpse of hope, he reached out
To the porcelain lining, gave her wings to fly
She soared above the sorcerer, began to live
Saved the fragile girl inside.

# INNOCENCE

Why hide and run away from the pure innocence of love
To veil in a heart full of denial
Against everything that is real and true
In a world that is ceaselessly unknown.
The only wholeness to hang on to
Is pushed away
Through the everyday fear brought on through
Everyday existence.
Someday there will be the will to want
And the simple desire to need
The notion to crave the possible
What is real?
What is simply complex in a child's play —
Rather no reason to fortify this way.
True love should not be a challenge
To hang onto and keep
It is given, for
Innocence can one day show its passion.

# ONE TRIP

A light peers through the darkened curtains
Hanging down past the window sill
Outside a liquor store, an alley, a child running
Many after knife in hand.
She sees the train that left her off
To find what she wished she knew
What she was looking for.
A sad sight to an endless fight
Peering up into the sky, the clouds of darkness
Inside she crumbles in a corner crying into her hands
Contemplating now on where they've been
Wrapping never washed curtains
Around her body, the creation of genuine comfort.

# TRUE LOVE

Your kisses are like ribbons
That tickle my body
And wind about my mind
Capturing inside a fixation of your divine
Desire for my forever devotion.
To feel your softness, your touch
An embrace of the indescribable erg
Inside holding around my love—
And love
The simple endurances that tingle through our bodies
And join us as one
As you're feeling my calling
To what each other is knowing.

And now
I am found through
The affirmation of your eventuality
That held me ever so close.
Grace — the elegance
Of your purity for love
Is celebrated in the honour
Brought by your virtue
A completion of fulfilment
Left upon our souls, true love engages
Forever, always.

# BECOME

Encroach peacefully
Bashful
The climb of chance — self created
Shout out and become
More than ever witnessed
Experience the edge and go beyond.

# BROKEN

Deep inside my soul
Mate I thought you were
But how could you do that?
And be?
What I feared deep inside my soul
Mate I held you close
Then scared to let you hold me tight
And the tears streamed down
The little face
I tried to hold up high
When you put me low
Never leave my soul
Mate was that you?
Who made me cry?

# HIS FIXATION

She was glazed everlasting
The canvas wore its tare not to fade
Design her beauty
Two most precious eyes — first to see
Hoist her inner exquisite
And he called out her name, in painting
Always at a persist: "I will find beauty someday"
As then it came alive
He searched her canvas eyes once more
Just then believing his imaginary
Now became his reality.

# BIZZARE

Why would there ever be snow
Storms in April?
Showers float to spring
Up flowers
Buzzing bees and weeds.
How could there be an ice
Blizzard in April?
Yellow grass receives
Its green
Hoppers and silent poppers
Seasons changing.

# HINDSIGHT

Too many moments I thought it was real
I felt it to be, but knew it couldn't be — you and me.
Mesmerized, fluttering hearts firing
And then capsized — seized by the reality
That my emotions will be burnt
Before a chance to ignite what I cannot deny.
Now knowing the right move
From the beginning
I also know it would have been
A different ending.

# REVELATION

There was a time when
Everything felt like an adventure
And it was — not being experienced before
The first intensity
Replaced over years of events
To be a pattern where the ultimate question still
Not discovered — the dilemma
Where do we go?
To some nowhere- utter abyss
Everything we cannot see
But only for the human eye
Capturing completely nothing
Of black endless drift-
The spiritual sense
A higher passing tense
Accepting of, believing and
Meaning the receiving of first time sight.

# SOME DAY FOUND

Tried to be beautiful
And could not seem to meet
That invisible standard.
Waiting alone to be rescued
The prayers unanswered
And searching for meaning
Between the lines
Of the words I cannot read so clearly.
What is the solution?
For what I should be doing
Can silence find clarity?
Because that is all I have.
Wanting to be found
By the one I look into their eyes
Seeing my symmetrical half
Good night to the shining armour
That never came.

# DECISIONS

Categorize what is right and wrong
Compile anything useful to the mind
Finding the answers to what is real
What is not — what is definite?
Is anything?
What secures the creditability?
When taking a chance, anything could be
Everything or simply nothing.
Let go of what you think you know
Reach to break barriers — recreate the created.

# REFLECTION

Pouring and standing here alone
She is listening carefully to the coded
Pleading patterns of crashing water droplets
Calling out desperately wanting to be calm
An inside commotion
She blends with night time shadows
Her trench is the outside veranda
Engulfed in the sound of speechless
Roaming vehicles—a distant highway
Off on riveting road in search to reach
Everyday or extraordinary destinations—
Was hers to land beyond
The sliding glass doors
Response—to reunify
Join the separation
To form blood connection
Once perceived as the end
Now the beginning
A mark in the journey
The unknown soon to be known.

# JUDGEMENT

Common grounds habituate humanity in a state
Referred to as home
The earth settles amongst
Bearing our dignity
Giving turf to stand tall
As man and woman
Shall rise to report
Accountability of individuality
Testify the testimony
Of goodness against evils
The direction given against deceiving
Patterns — our faith
To be recognizable
A distinction amongst the body form
Deliverance to, an awaiting home.

# TRAVELER IN LIFE

The dreariness surrounded inside
The soul of one quite innocent cretin
Emerging through life to find a passion
Lurking his way.
A path of uncarved shredded knots
In need of a cipher
To aid in the clearing
Of how the cretin became the traveler
Destined to be someone — anyone.
The gore he held that bared his face
Stood not the way to find his living
Exterior to interior its symbolism spread
Plagued him and contained — hidden within the cretin.

# DREAMS

Inspire to transpire truth
Possibilities turn into realities
When the horizon given, locate the source
Search to select choices, discover the ultimate decision
A pathway presented through limitless opportunities
No restrictions — only self structured
Soar above this constriction
Or the crucified daily pattern
Will play out in shifting slides
The concrete constraint bearing against what you feel is right
Or wrong, prove against and beyond.

# ANGELS

Did you hear that whisper?
Softly tracing itself through passing thoughts
Do you feel a slight presence?
Calming itself over your embrace
They have traveled amongst us
Through you and I
Speaking in tongues
And representing images.
The message has been sent
For do not be afraid
A human cure —
Rested in hope
Holding your faith
When all is lost
In the wings
You do not recognize.